Come Over

by Liza Charlesworth

ISBN: 978-0-545-25637-7

Illustrated by Anne Kennedy
Designed by Maria Lilja • Colored by Ka-Yeon Kim-Li
Copyright © 2010 by Liza Charlesworth

SCHOLASTIC

Come over and see my chair.

Come over and see my table.

Come over and see my lamp.

Come over and see my tub.

Come over and see my couch.

Come over and see my dresser.

Come over and see my dollhouse!